ISBN 0-8109-1150-7

Published in 1989 by Harry N. Abrams, Incorporated, New York

A Times Mirror Company

Printed and bound in Hong Kong

Lewis Carroll

JABBERWOCKY

from *Through the Looking Glass*

Illustrated by Graeme Base

Harry N. Abrams, Inc., Publishers, New York

WAS brillig, and the slithy toves
　　Did gyre and gimble in the wabe:
　　　All mimsy were the borogoves,
　　　　And the mome raths outgrabe.

EWARE the Jabberwock, my son!
The jaws that bite, the claws that catch!
Beware the Jubjub bird, and shun
The frumious Bandersnatch!"

E TOOK his vorpal sword in hand:
    Long time the manxome foe he sought—
    So rested he by the Tumtum tree,
    And stood awhile in thought.

And, as in uffish thought he stood,
The Jabberwock, with eyes of flame,
    Came whiffling through the tulgey wood,
    And burbled as it came!

NE, two! One, two! And through and through
The vorpal blade went snicker-snack!
He left it dead, and with its head
He went galumphing back.

"And, hast thou slain the Jabberwock?
Come to my arms, my beamish boy!
O frabjous day! Callooh! Callay!"
He chortled in his joy.

'T was brillig, and the slithy toves
    Did gyre and gimble in the wabe:
    All mimsy were the borogoves,
      And the mome raths outgrabe.